HOW TO LIVE A GOOD LIFE

SMOOTH SAILING FOREVER

LEARN THE TIPS AND TRICKS FOR AN INDEPENDENT FUTURE

Awais Hobbs

Table of Contents

PART 1 5
Chapter 1: The Things That Matter.. 6
Chapter 2: The Power of Contentment 10
Chapter 3: **Start Working On Your Dreams Today**...................... 12
Chapter 4: Why You Are Amazing.. 16
Chapter 5: When It Is Time To Say No To Things 18
Chapter 6: Stop Setting The Wrong Goals..................................... 21
Chapter 7: How To Be A Better Listener....................................... 24
Chapter 8: Discovering Your Strengths and Weaknesses 27
Chapter 9: Learning To Trust Others 30
Chapter 10: Discomfort Is Temporary 32
PART 2 37
Chapter 1: How To Achieve True Happiness................................ 38
Chapter 2: How To Rid Yourself of Distraction 42
Chapter 3: How to Learn Faster... 45
Chapter 4: *Don't Set The Wrong Goals*.. 48
Chapter 5: It's Okay To Feel Uncertain 51
Chapter 6: Deal With Your Fears Now.. 54
Chapter 7: If You Commit to Nothing, You'll Be Distracted By Everything 57
Chapter 8: How To Improve Your Communication Skills......... 60
Chapter 9: Overcoming Tiredness and Lethargy......................... 65
Chapter 10: Bounce Back From Failure.. 68
PART 3 71
Chapter 1: The Struggle With Time.. 72
Chapter 2: Friendship The Key To Happiness 74
Chapter 3: Get in the Water (Stop wasting time)......................... 77
Chapter 4: When It Is Time To Let Go and Move On (Career)........ 79

Chapter 5: Being Open To Opportunities For Social Events 82
Chapter 6: Trust The Process 85
Chapter 7: Pressures of Social Media 88
Chapter 8: Share Your Wisdom with the World 91
Chapter 9: The Lure of Wanting Luxury Items 95
Chapter 10: The 5 Second Rule 98

PART 1

Chapter 1:
The Things That Matter

Today we're going to talk about a topic that I am very passionate about. Passionate because it has helped to guide each and every decision that I make on a daily basis. Having this constant reminder of the things that matter will put things in perspective for us - to eliminate the things that are taking up our time for the wrong reasons and to focus on the things that we actually want deep down in our hearts.

With that in mind, let's begin.

How many of you can safely say that you know what truly matters in life? How do you define living a successful and fulfilling life? Is it by having a certain net worth? Is it by living a stress-free life? Is it seeing the world? Is it by serving a defined number of people? Is it by having 10 life-long friends that you can count on? Is it by having a certain number of kids? Or have you not really thought about what you really want out of life yet?

Before we can really gear our actions towards the direction that we want to lead it, we must first know exactly what those specific things we want to achieve are.

The things that matter in my life vary over time as I get older and wiser. When I was young I used to think getting good grades, getting into a good university, and getting a good and stable job was all that really mattered, but I have soon come to realize that family, friends, and having people to hang out with were way more important than simply making money. There was a point in my life that I was so driven by money that I created a huge imbalance in my life by spending 99% of my time on my career. This lopsided drive caused me to neglect friendships, relationships, and soon people associated me with always being too busy for anything. I gradually stopped hanging out with anyone altogether. At first it was okay as I thought "hey, I finally have time to do whatever I want" and I don't have to be disturbed by meetups that would disrupt my workflow. But over time, I felt a gaping hole opening up somewhere deep inside that I could not seem to fill. I suddenly realized that I had successfully isolated myself from any and all relationships. This isolation felt increasingly lonely for me. I felt that I had no one to talk to when I was feeling down, no one to share my struggles with, no one to walk this journey with, and I knew I needed to do something about it. It was only after I started reconnecting with my friends did I truly feel alive again. Having friends brought me more joy than money ever did or could. There's a saying that you can't buy happiness; the same is true for friendships - you can't buy them either. They have to be earned and built with trust and loyalty.

For those of you who are so career focused and money-minded, I share from experience that the destination may not be pretty if you do not have friends or family to share it with. Sure you may afford a penthouse or a Ferrari, but what does it really mean? Sure you have a nice view and a fast ride, but can you share your life with it? When you are old and frail, can your house and car support you physically and emotionally? Don't make the same mistake I did for a good 3 years of my life. It was enough time for me to feel completely alone. No amount of acquiring things could fill that hole no matter how hard I tried. Sure I had the fanciest Apple products, my iPad, iPhone, MacBook, iMac, AirPods, the list goes on. Sure I could "make friends" with these shiny objects by using them everyday. But over time it just reminded me more and more that I had replaced people with gadgets, that I had replaced humans with Siri. It was really really sad honestly.

Having friends that don't judge you or who don't care whether you have money or not, those are the real friends that you know you can count on. And I urge those of you who have neglected this big part to start reconnecting old friends or finding new ones altogether who share the same interests as you. Golf buddies, tennis buddies, karaoke buddies, these are good places to start searching for friends and getting the ice broken.

If starting a family is something that you really want in life, have you begun searching for a partner and planning how and when you expect that to happen for you? Sure many of us think we may have a lot of time to do after we get our career going, but how many of us have heard stories of people who just never got off the bandwagon because they've become too busy with their careers? That maybe getting pregnant just never seems like the right time because you don't want to jeopardize your job. Or maybe that you never even got around to dating at all by the time you are 35 because you've become too busy being a general manager of your company. If having a career is the most important thing to you, then by all means go full steam ahead to achieve that goal. However if family is something of great significance to you, you may want to consider starting that timeline right now instead of waiting. Remember the goal is to focus on the things that truly matter. If having a loving spouse who you can grow old with and having say 2 kids who can support you when you are old is what you really want, maybe waiting isn't such a good idea. Finding love takes practice. You will meet frogs along the way and it takes time to grow a lasting relationship. Sure you can rush a marriage if time is of the essence, but is that ideal? Personally I believe a strong relationship takes 2-3 years to build. Do you have that type of runway to play with? Don't work yourself to death at your job only to find yourself rich and alone. Regret will come after for sure.

Whatever else you have defined as the things that matter to you, make sure that you never neglect those priorities. Sometimes life gets so busy and hectic that we forget to stop and refresh ourselves on what we really want to get out of life. It is all too easy for us to operate on autopilot - To set an alarm, go to work, gym, go home, take dinner, sleep, and repeat the day all over again. For weekends, we may be so exhausted from work that we just end up sleeping or wasting our weekend away only to begin the same routine again on Monday.

There's plenty of time for work decades down the road, but dating relationships and friendships may not have that runway of time.

So I challenge each and everyone of you to clearly define what the things that matter mean to you and to take consistent action in these areas day in and out until you can safely say you've already checked them off your bucket list. Take care and I'll see you in the next one.

Chapter 2:
The Power of Contentment

Today we're going to talk about why contentment is possibly a much more attainable and sustainable alternative than trying to achieve happiness.

As we have briefly gone through in the previous video, happiness is a state of mind that is fleeting and never truly lasts for too very long before the opposing forces of sadness and feelings of boredom start creeping in.

Happiness is a limited resource that needs energy and time to build, and we can never really be truly happy all the time. But what about the notion of contentment?

Contentment is a state of feeling that you are satisfied with the current situation and it need not go beyond that. When we say we are contented with our circumstances, with our jobs, with our friends, family, and relationships, we are telling ourselves that we have enough, and that we can and should be grateful for the things we have instead of feeling lacking in the things we don't.

Many a times when i ask myself if i am happy about something, be it a situation that I had found myself in, or the life that I am living, majority of the time the answer is a resounding no. And it is not because I am unhappy per se, but if i were to ask myself honestly, I can't bring myself to say that yes absolutely that all is great and that I am 100$% truly happy with everything. I have to say that this is my own personal experience and it may not be an accurate representation of how you see life.

However, if i were to reframe and ask myself this question of "Am I Contented with my life?" I can with absolute confidence say yes I am. I may not have everything in the world, but i can most definitely say I am contented with my job, my friends, my family, my career, my relationships, and my health and body. That I do not need to keep chasing perfection in order to be contented with myself.

You will find that as you ask yourself more and more if you are contented, and if the answer is mostly a yes, you will gradually feel a shift towards a feeling that actually life is pretty good. And that your situation is actually very favourable. Yes you may not be happy all the time, but then again who is? As long as you are contented 90% of the time, you have already won the game of life. And when you pair contentment with a feeling of gratefulness of the things you have, you will inevitably feel a sense of happiness without having to ask yourself that question or be trying to chase it down on a daily basis.

Many a times when I looked at my current situation to see if I was on the right track, I look around me and I feel that whilst there may be areas that I am lacking and certainly needs improvement, in the grand scheme of things, I am pretty well off and i am contented.

So I challenge all of you today to look at your life in a different perspective. Start asking yourself the right question of "are you contented", and if by any chance you are not majority of the time, look at what you can do to change things up so that you do feel that life is indeed great and worth living.

I wish you guys all the success in life and I'll see you in the next one. Take care.

Chapter 3:
Start Working On Your Dreams Today

When did you get up today? What was your day like? What did you achieve today? Did any of that matter?

Maybe it didn't because you don't have any dreams to work towards, or maybe that you've forgotten what they are altogether.

To have a dream is to have a direction in life. To have a dream means you have something bigger than yourself that you want to achieve.

Everyone gets at least one chance in their life to actually go and pursue that dream, but few recognize that until it is too late. It is too late to regret when you are on your deathbed wondering what could have been. That is when it is too late to work on your dreams. When you have no more time left.

The Moment to start working On your dreams is right here right now.

We repeat our failures every day but never learn. We get depressed every day but never communicate. We get bullied every day, but never fight back. Why?

Is it because we can't do it? No, Definitely Not! We can do it whenever we want. We can do it today. We can do it the next minute. We just lack Ambition!

Every day someone achieves something big. Some more than often, others maybe not their whole life. But the outcome is **not** determined by **fate**, but with **Effort**.

All the billionaires you see today started out with a few dollars just like you and me. They just had the guts to pursue their dream no matter what the cost is. They all had a vision of something bigger. They went full throttle even when everyone around them expected them to fail. Even when they met with struggles that hit them harder than the last, they were still focused on the dream. Never did they once lesson the effort.

No two persons are born the same. Not the same face, color, intelligence, or fate. But what's common for every human being is the built-in trait to strive for a goal once they are determined enough. Doesn't matter if it's food for the next meal or success for the times to come.

The struggle is real, it always was, it always will be. The world wouldn't be what it is today if it weren't for the struggle man has gone through over the centuries. The struggle is the most real definition of life in this world. But that doesn't mean it's a bad one.

Our parents struggled to make us a better person. They put in their best effort to watch us succeed in our dreams. Their parents did the same for them and their parents before them.

This is what makes life a cycle of inherited struggle and hardships. Nobody asks to struggle through a hard life, but we can all turn the hard life into a meaningful one. The life that we all should expect to eventually achieve only if we keep the cycle running and if we keep putting in the effort.

How then do we actually work towards our dreams? By focusing on the things that matter each and every day, again and again, until that mountain has been conquered. Don't forget to enjoy the journey, because it could well be the best part of the trip up top.

You never know what the next moment has in it for you. You can never predict the future, but you can always hope for a better one. You only get the right to hope if you did what was meant to be done today. It's your lawful right to reap the fruit if you took care of sowing the seeds faithfully and diligently all through the year.

The motivation behind this continuous grind of time in search of that Dream lies in your past. You cannot achieve those dreams until you start treasuring the lessons of your past and become a person who is always willing to go beyond.

You can't simply depend on hope to get something done. You have to reach the point where start obsessing over that goal, that thing, that DREAM. When you start obsessing, you start working, you start seeing the possibilities and you just keep going. If you don't get up then you WILL miss the moment. The moment that could have made all the difference in the world. If you don't act upon that impulse, you might never get that inspiration ever again. And that will be the moment you will always regret for the rest of your life.

Remember that your whole life is built on millions of tiny decisions. A decision to just act on one of those moments can transform your life completely. These moments often test you too. But only for an inch more before you find eternal glory. So don't wait for someone else to do it for you. Get up, buckle up, and start doing. Because only you Can!

Chapter 4:
Why You Are Amazing

When was the last time you told yourself that you were amazing? Was it last week, last month, last year, or maybe not even once in your life?

As humans, we always seek to gain validation from our peers. We wait to see if something that we did recently warranted praise or commendation. Either from our colleagues, our bosses, our friends, or even our families. And when we don't receive those words that we expect them to, we think that we are unworthy, or that our work just wasn't good enough. That we are lousy and under serving of praise.

With social media and the power of the internet, these feelings have been amplified. For those of us that look at the likes on our Instagram posts or stories, or the number of followers on Tiktok, Facebook, or Snapchat, we allow ourselves to be subjected to the validation of external forces in order to qualify our self-worth. Whether these are strangers who don't know you at all, or whoever they might be, their approval seems to matter the most to us rather than the approval we can choose to give ourselves.

We believe that we always have to up our game in order to seek happiness. Everytime we don't get the likes, we let it affect our mood for the rest of the day or even the week.

Have you ever thought of how wonderful it is if you are your best cheerleader in life? If the only validation you needed to seek was from yourself? That you were proud of the work you put out there, even if the world disagrees, because you know that you have put your heart and soul into the project and that there was nothing else you could have done better in that moment when you were producing that thing?

Smooth Sailing Forever

I am here to tell you that you are amazing because only you have the power to choose to love yourself unconditionally. You have the power to tell yourself that you are amazing. and that you have the power to look into yourself and be proud of how far you came in life. To be amazed by the things that you have done up until this point, things that other people might not have seen, acknowledged, or given credit to you for. But you can give that credit to yourself. To pat yourself on the back and say "I did a great job".

I believe that we all have this ability to look inwards. That we don't need external forces to tell us we are amazing because deep down, we already know we are.

If nobody else in the world loves you, know that I do. I love your courage, your bravery, your resilience, your heart, your soul, your commitment, and your dedication to live out your best life on this earth. Tell yourself each and everyday that you deserve to be loved, and that you are loved.

Go through life fiercely knowing that you don't need to seek happiness, validations, and approval from others. That you have it inside you all along and that is all you need to keep going.

Chapter 5:
When It Is Time To Say No To Things

In my previous video I talked about the joys of saying yes to things and taking time out of your work to enjoy life and hanging out with friends. And I encouraged everyone to put themselves in favourable positions where they could say yes to things. However the question that we have to answer for ourselves today is "when should we draw the line and when does yes actually stops yielding benefits and instead could harm our progress towards the goals that we have set for ourselves?

To answer this question, I will bring it back to my own life once again to try and give it some perspective. As all of you know by now, I was working hard in prioritising social activities as I felt that there was a huge imbalance in my work life and my play life. At one point in my life, work was a full on 99% and play was a measly 1%. And simple math would tell you that it wasn't very healthy at all.

But as I started baking in more fun activities into my schedule, the percentage difference grew smaller and smaller. And it became so easy to simply choose fun over work that i actually started spending less time on my work than I did on friends. And similarly, simple math would tell u that too much of a good thing might not actually be that good after all.

As an entrepreneur, I am what I put into my business. And less time spent on my work also meant that I started falling behind on deadlines that I had set for myself at the beginning of the year. I became increasingly complacent and my income started to stagnate. It was at the point that i knew again that I needed to change something. I needed to tweak and prioritise my time more wisely. Carving time out for work whilst also balancing friends and sports for health and fitness purposes.

Smooth Sailing Forever

For those working a 9-5 job, there is a clear definition between work time and play time, but as as someone who is self employed, that line is often blurred. And without proper structure, commitment, and time management, one can easily fall into the trap of simply justifying time off. There is no boss breathing down my neck and that could be a good or bad thing depending on how you look at it.

You see, life is all about constant adjustments and fine tuning until we reach an equilibrium that we can say is the perfect balance. That ratio need not necessarily be 50/50, it could be any ratio that you decide it should be. I decided that I needed to spend 70% of my time on work at 30% of my time on social activities. And my next goal was to restructure my time accordingly. that meant that I needed to learn how to say no or grab a rain check when friends asked me out.

I also had to figure out what kind of work and play schedule would work for me. And the easiest was to look at my calender to carve out blocks of time that I know i would be the most productive and to just work as much as i could. If someone were to ask me out on those blocks of time, i needed to have the discipline to say no and to ask for a reschedule into one of the slots of that I have set aside for play.

You see I know myself better than anyone, and I know that if I scheduled play before work, 99% of the time, I would just end up spending the whole day playing and then regretting after that I had not done any work at all. So knowing yourself and how you function is key here in deciding when to say no or yes to things.

As I became more disciplined in saying no, I saw my productivity at work start to pic. R Rk up again. And I was back on track to reaching my goals again. I also slowly clawed my productivity back up to 70%. And I felt that it was the perfect balance for me.

So the takeaway from today's video is that you need to figure out what your goals are and exactly how much time you should or need to spend on your work to justify to yourselves that you have put in enough work to move the needle forward in your life

Smooth Sailing Forever

without sacrificing time with friends. You need to be busy enough to be productive but not too busy that you come across as unavailable all the time. And you need to know who you are as a person and what exactly the balance is that you need to ensure that you are covering all areas of your life and that you are satisfied and happy with that decision.

So I challenge each and everyone of you today to take stock of your time, how you are spending them, what your goals are, so that when an invite comes, you know exactly whether to say no or yes without feelings of regret.

I hope you learned something new today and i wish you all the best in your endeavours. Take care and I'll see you in the next one.

Chapter 6:
Stop Setting The Wrong Goals

Setting the wrong goals will lead to disappointment in success.
Chances are you are aiming too low and
will not be satisfied with the outcome.
The outcome and the reason for
it must be clear before you begin.
Will the result make you satisfied?
Will you enjoy the journey to the result?
Your goal should encompass these questions
to make sure you are not setting the wrong goals.

You may be setting the wrong goals due to the expectations of others.
The goals you set should be personal to you -
something where you can enjoy the process and the result.
Is your goal likely to happen based on your current actions?
What could you do to make it more likely?
If you set the wrong goals you will end up doing a whole lot of work you
don't like doing for a result you don't want.

Start at the end in your mind.
What would the end result look, taste and feel like?
With that you can imagine the process.
Can you do that work?

Smooth Sailing Forever

Would you enjoy that work?
Or would the reality fall short of your current expectations.

Life is chess not checkers.
The grand masters of success play 10 years ahead.
Thinking about how their actions today will
influence their lives ten years from now .
What's your 10 year goal?
What are your first steps?
Start at the end and work it back to now in your mind.

If you can envision the goal and paths to it
the battle is half won and you will have clarity over your goals.
Setting the wrong goals decreases your motivation to attain them.
You can only attain your motivation if your why is strong enough.

What are you aiming for and why?
If your clarity is strong enough you will
feel the goal as if it is already real.
You can then confirm it is the right goal for you.

If you only feel half-hearted about something it is not for you
and it is probably a waste of your time.
It's better to go all out for something you really want
than to easily obtain something you don't.

The right goal for you will probably feel unrealistic at first.

People will probably tell you it is.
But you know that it really isn't.
If it's on your mind constantly then it
stands a good chance that it is the right goal for you.

You must think clearly about every aspect of your life
and the goal you wish to obtain.
Something that fits you and your true desires.

Your goal should be something that will make you happy as often as possible and give you the kind of financial life you want.
Never set goals because someone else thinks that is what you should be doing.
Only you know what you should be doing,
go after that and never accept anything less.
Gain clarity on your goals before you act.
Make sure it's something that will make you happy in the process and the results that come from it.

Chapter 7:
How To Be A Better Listener

Today we're going to talk about a topic that could potentially help you not only in your relationships, such as with your boyfriend, girlfriend, and best friends, but also in your workplace with your colleagues, peers, and your bosses or understudies.

Why is being a better listener so vital you might ask? It is simple, because as humans, we all want to be heard. And we all want to feel like people are listening to us and understanding us not just on a superficial level, but emotionally as well. We have a desire to share our pains, sorrows, unhappiness, and even happiness and special events with people who are willing to lend a listening ear to us. And we instantly feel connected to the person who is listening to us.

We are given a mouth and two ears for a reason. I know it sounds silly, but I have to repeat again here that we are social creatures, and we try to find connections with people as much as we can. And there is no better way to be connected than with someone who are willing to spend the time to hear us.

Think back to a time when someone actually told u, thanks for listening to my problems. Either through text or in person. How did you feel? And how did they react to you being a good listener? Were they appreciative? Or were they nonchalant about it. I would bet that they were appreciative and they know that they had found someone that they could count on to tell their problems too. Of course u dont want it to be a habit that someone constantly "bitches" to you about every single thing that is going wrong in their life. You have to learn how to draw the line there. But generally if it is a one-off problem, I'm sure you guys became better friends, partners, or lovers.

Now think back to a time when someone told u off for not listening to their problems. Where you constantly interjected their sharing with advice without letting them finish what they had to say. This would most likely be your partner who would get angry at you, but what were their feelings at that point? Did they say "you're not listening to me" or "You dont understand?". That has happened to me before on multiple occasions when i tried to impose my ideas on a situation thinking that that is what the person wanted, advice. But in reality, they know how to solve the problem but they just want someone that they could vent to. To share their story and then move on.

So if people have been telling u that you're not a good listener, or that you don't listen or that u dont understand what they want, more often than not, the problem is that you did not just let the person say what they wanted to say, to have their piece. Your job is not to dish out advice, but just to sit there, interested, and ask them to go on. And at the end of it give out a hug rather than an advice.

So you must be wondering how this could link to your colleagues. Well for one, you have to be a good person to begin with in order for people to trust u with work related matters. If colleagues don't trust you, they won't be open to sharing with you problems they might have with their bosses or other issues that they need to vent about. But if they do trust you, and know you are not the type who will go round spreading gossip but rather is a good genuine person with a good heart and a listening ear, you have just gotten yourself an ally at the workplace. And you would have built a friendship at work that could last you a lifetime. You never know when these connections that you have made would provide you with future job opportunities, whether these colleagues could become your bosses in another company one day. But you want to keep your colleagues close to you and you want to retain their respect, trust, and be professional. Vice versa, you may also find a listening ear in a colleague that you can share your problems with. But i must warn you that sometimes people can be disingenuous so you've gotta be careful to not overshare information that could be used against you. Especially through messages where they can be screen captured and could get you in trouble.

On the flip side, Now I want you to use this power for good and not as insider information to manipulate your way up to corporate ladder, do what you will with your gift but karma does come around. And if you have ill intentions for being a good listener, it will come back to bite you someday. I am certain of it. People will know you are a faker and your reputation will precede you.

As you can clearly, being a good listener has immense pay offs for your personal and professional career. And learning to have an open ear could help you gain many potential friends at work and at play. How you respond when people share their stories and having a good character yourself personally also plays an important role in actually keeping these friends close to you as well, but being a good listener is a nice way to start.

I hope you learned something valuable today and I'll see you in the next one. Take care!

Chapter 8:
Discovering Your Strengths and Weaknesses

Today we're going to talk about a very simple yet important topic that hopefully brings about some self discovery about who you really are. By the end of this video i wish to help you find out what areas you are weak at so that maybe you could work on those, and what your strengths are so that you can play to them and lean into them more for greater results in your career and life in general.

We should all learn to accept our flaws as much as we embrace our strengths. And we have to remember that each of us are unique and we excel in different areas. Some of us are more artistic, some visionary, some analytical, some hardworking, some lazy, what matters is that we make these qualities work for us in our own special way.

Let's start by identifying your weaknesses. For those of you that have watched enough of my videos, you would know that i encourage all of you to take a pen to write things down. So lets go through this exercise real quick. Think of a few things that people have told you that you needed to work on, be it from your Teachers, your friends, your family, or whoever it may be.

How many of these weaknesses would you rate as significantly important that it would affect your life in a drastic way if you did not rectify it? I want you to put them at the top of your list. Next spend some time to reflect and look in the mirror. Be honest with yourself and identify the areas about yourself that you know needs some work.

Now I want you to take some time to identity your strengths. Repeat the process from above, what are the things people have told you about yourself that highlighted certain qualities about you? Whether that you're very outgoing, friendly, a great singer, a good team player, very diligent. I want you to write as many of these down as you can. No matter how big or small these strengths are, I want you to write down as many as you can.

Now I want you to also place your 3 biggest strengths at the top of the list. As I believe these are the qualities that best represent who you are as a person.

Now that you've got these 2 lists. I want you to compare them. Which list is longer? the one with strengths or weaknesses? If you have more weaknesses, that's okay, it just means that there is more room for improvement. If you have more strengths, thats good.

What we are going to do with this list now is to now make it a mission to improve our weaknesses and play heavily into our strengths for the foreseeable future. You see, our strengths are strengths for a reason, we are simply naturally good at it. Whether it be through genetics, or our personalities, or the way we have been influenced by the world. We should all try to showcase our strengths as much as we can. It is hard for me to say exactly what that is, but I believe that you will know how you maximise the use of your talent. Whether it be serving others, performing for others, or even doing specific focused tasks. Simply do more of it. Put yourself in more situations where you can practice these strengths. And keep building on it. It will take little effort but yield tremendous results.

As for your weaknesses, I want you to spend some time on the top 3 that you have listed so far. As these could be the areas that have been holding you back the most. Making improvements in these areas could be the breakthrough that you need to become a much better person and could see you achieving a greater level success than if you had just left them alone.

Smooth Sailing Forever

I challenge each and everyone of you to continually play to your strengths, sharpening them until they are sharp as a knife, while working on smoothening the rough edges of your weaknesses. So that they may balance out your best qualities.

I hope that you have learned something today. Keep working on yourself and I believe in each and every one of you. Take care and I'll see you in the next one.

Chapter 9:
Learning To Trust Others

Today we're going to talk about a topic that has the potential to make or break your working relationships or personal relationships with others.

Trust is something that consistently ranks on the top of relationship goals and it has very good reasons for that. Without trust there is basically no foundation. When you can't trust someone, it basically means that you don't believe they can be left alone without your supervision. If you don't trust someone to do the work you have passed along to them, basically it means you are either micro-managing them all day long or that you might just end up doing the work entirely yourself because you don't believe that they can do a job up to your expectations. How many of you have experienced bosses who are micro-managers like that? Basically it either means that they think they can do a better job or that they don't trust you to do the work at all. And we all hate bosses who are like that. Look into mirror like that now, are you doing that to someone at your workplace now?

If you don't trust someone in a relationship, basically you don't believe that they can't be left to their own devices either if they are out of your sight. You start to worry about what they might do when you're gone. If a partner has cheated on you before, I bet that trust has probably gone out the window and it might take a lot of time and energy to actually start trusting that person again. If you don't trust a friend, you might not want to tell them secrets for fear that they may go round sharing it with others without your consent. That plays into the concept of trustworthiness as well. It all comes in a package.

To build trust, we have to earn it. With our actions we can show others that we can be trusted with information, secrets, work, to be faithful, and to do right thing at all times. But trust works both ways as well. If we want people to trust us, we must be willing to extend the trust to others as well. If others have displayed level of competency, we need to start learning to trust that they can get the work done without breathing down their necks all times of the day. If however they come back with shoddy work, maybe you might want to keep a closer eye on them before you feel that their work is up to your standards.

Let others prove to you otherwise by giving them the benefit of the doubt first and then assessing their abilities after.

When you show others that you trust them to do a task, more often than not they will feel a sense of urgency and responsibility to get the work done properly and promptly so that they can show you that they are capable. To show you that they are competent and worthy of the trust that you have placed in them. When you can learn to trust can you truly let go and live life freely. Always having to micro-manage others can not only hurt your reputation as "that guy" but also allow you to have more time do focus on areas where your attention is really required. When you can learn to trust can you truly expand and grow a team, business, company, friendships, and relationships.

I challenge each and everyone of you to learn to trust others and not feel like you have to manage everyone around you to the granular level. If you feel that you have trust issues, for whatever reason, consider working on it or maybe even seeking help. Trust issues usually stems from a past traumatic event or experience that may have impacted your ability to trust again. If so you may one to dig deeper to discover the root of the problem and work through it till the feeling goes away.

Take care and I'lll see you in the next one.

Chapter 10:
Discomfort Is Temporary

It's easy to get hopeless when things get a little overwhelming. It's easy to give up because you feel you don't have the strength or resources to continue. But where you stop is actually the start you have been looking for since the beginning.

Do you know what you should do when you are broken? You should relish it. You should use it. Because if you know you are broken, congratulations, you have found your limitations.

Now as you know what stopped you last time, you can work towards mending it. You can start to reinforce the breach and you should be able to fill in the cracks in no time.

Life never repeats everything. One day you feel the lowest and the next might bring you the most unpredictable gifts.

The world isn't all sunshine and rainbows. It is a very mean and nasty place to be in. But what can you do now when you are in it? Nothing? Never!

You have to endure the pain, the stress, the discomfort till you are comfortable with the discomfort. It doesn't make any sense, right? But listen to me.

You have a duty towards yourself. You have a duty towards your loved ones. You are expected to rise above all odds and be something no one has ever been before you. I know it might be a little too much to ask for, but, you have to understand your purpose.

Your purpose isn't just to sit on your back and the opportunities and blessings keep coming, knocking at your door, just so you can give up one more time and turn them down.

Things are too easy to reject and neglect but always get hard when you finally step up and go for them. But remember, every breathtaking view is from the top of a hill, but the trek to the top is always tiring. But when you get to the top, you find every cramp worth it.

If you are willing to put yourself through anything, discomfort and temporary small intervals of pain won't affect you in any way. As long as you believe that the experience will bring you to a new level.

If you are interested in the unknown, then you have to break barriers and cross your limits. Because every path that leads to success is full of them. But then and only then you will find yourself in a place where you are unbreakable.

You need to realize that your life is better than most people out there. You need to embrace the pain because all this is temporary. But when you are finally ready to embrace the pain, you are already on your way to a superior being.

Life is all about taking stands because we all get all kinds of blows. But we always need to dig in and keep fighting till we have found the gems or have found our last breath.

The pain and discomfort will subside one day, but if you quit, then you are already on the end of your rope.

Fight Is The Reward

There are times in our lives when we feel blocked out. When we feel the darkness coming in. When we see the sun going down and seemingly never coming back up. When the winds feel tougher and everything coming in your way puts you down like a storm.

No matter how big and how defiant you get, life will always find a new way to knock you down.

You will often find yourself in a place where you have nowhere to go, but straight. And that straight path isn't always the easiest too. It has all these ridges and peaks or a long ditch. So you finally come to realize that the only way out is a challenge itself and you can't bow out because there is no other way around.

I want you to understand the concept of fight and struggle. The success stories and breakthroughs we all hear are mostly just 2 parts; its 90% work and 10% fight.

We all work and we all work hard. But the defining moment of our journey is the final fight we go through.

The work we put in gets us to the bottom of the final barrier but the effort we need to summit the peak is the fight we put in and finally get the breakthrough. But fighting isn't easy. It is the hardest part of your journey to success.

The fight you need to put in isn't just the Xs and O's. The true fight is your mental toughness. It's your sheer will to keep going and keep pushing because you are just around the corner for the ultimate success.

You are just on the verge of finding the best reward of your life. You are on the cusp of seeing and enjoying your happiest moments. Because you have finally found your dreams and you have finally fulfilled your purpose in life.

Now is the time to rise and give up the feeling of giving up. Now is the time to get on top of your challenges. Now is the time to sweat and get over that pain.

This is the moment you need to be at your best. This is the time you need your A-game. This is the time to defy all odds and go all in. Because the finals moments need the final straw of strength and effort in your body.

Make a decision and become your own light. Believe in yourself like you have never before and you will never look back.

So if you ask me again why is fighting worth it. It's because your attitude makes you win long before you have even set the foot in the battleground. It's your will to keep going that makes you stand out even before getting into the spotlight.

You don't win a fight when you fight, you win a fight before the fight even begins. Your ultimate reward is the collection of all your efforts and resilience.

PART 2

Chapter 1:
How To Achieve True Happiness

How many of us actually know what happiness really is? And how many of us spend our whole lives searching for it but never seem to be happy?

I want to share with you my story today of how i stumbled upon true happiness and how you can achieve the same for yourself in your life.

Many of us go through the motion of trying to earn money because we think the more money we have, the better our lives will be. We chase the dream of increasing our earning power so that we can afford to buy nicer and more expensive things. And we believe that when we have more money, our happiness level will increase as well and we will be filled with so much money and happiness that we can finally stop chasing it.

Now I just wanna say, Yes, for those who come from a not so affluent background where they have a family to feed and basic needs have to be met to in order for them to survive, having a monetary goal to work towards is truly commendable as their drive, motivation, and sole purpose comes from supporting their family. Their sense of achievement, joy, and happiness comes from seeing their loved ones attaining basic needs and then go on to achieve success later in life at the expense of their time and energy. But they are more than okay with that and they do so with a willing heart, mind, and soul. You might even say that these people have achieved true happiness. Not because they are chasing more money, but because they are using that money to serve a greater purpose other than themselves.

But what about the rest of us who seemingly have everything we could ever want but never seem to be happy? We work hard at our jobs every single day waiting for our next promotion so that we can command a higher pay. And as our income grows, so does our appetite and desire for more expensive material things.

For guys we might chase that fancy new watch like rolex, omega, breitling, drooling over that model that always seem to be on a never-ending waitlist. And as we purchased one, feeling that temporary joy and satisfaction, we quickly look towards that next model as the shiny object we have starts to slowly fade. We lose our so-called happiness in time and We go back to work dreaming about that next watch just to feel that joy and excitement again. This could apply to other material things such as a shiny new technology gadgets smartphones, tv, and even cars.

For women, while might not be true for everyone, They might look towards that designer shoe, that branded handbag, ar that fancy jewellery that costs thousands of dollars to purchase but happily pay for it because they think it makes them feel better about ourselves. Or they could even use these purchases as retail therapy from their stressful lives and jobs.

Whatever these expensive purchases may be, we think that by spend our hard earned money on material things, it will bring us happiness and joy, but somehow it never does, and in most cases it is only temporary satisfactions.

That was exactly what happened with me. I kept chasing a higher income thinking it would bring me happiness. As a lover of technology, I always sought to buy the latest gadgets I could get my hands on. The excitement peaks and then fades. For me I realised that I had created an endless loop of trying to chase happiness but always coming up short.

One day I sat down and reflected on what exactly made me REALLY happy and I started writing down a list.

Smooth Sailing Forever

My List Came down to these in no particular order: Spending time with family, spending time with friends, helping others, having a purpose in life, being at peace with myself, working on my own dreams, singing and making music, exercising, being grateful, and finally being a loving person to others.

As I went through this list, I realised that hey, in none of the list did i write "making more money" or "buying more things". And it finally dawned on me that these are REALLY the things that made me truly happy. And only after I had defined these things did i actively choose to do more of them every single day.

I started spending more quality time with my friends and family, i started playing my favourite sport (Tennis) a few times a week, I chose to be grateful that I can even be alive on this earth, and I chose to be more loving and humble. Finally I also actively chose not to compare myself to people who were more "successful" than I was because comparing yourself to others can NEVER make you happy and will only make you feel inferior when you are not. Always remember that You are special, you are unique, and you are amazing.

After doing these things every single day, I had become a much happier person. It is all about perspective.

So what can you do to achieve happiness for yourself?

I recommend that you do the same thing I did which is to write down a list under the title "When Am I The Happiest?" or "When Was A Time When I Truly Felt Happy?" Start breaking down these memories as you recall your past, and down the essence of the memory. Everybody's list will be different as happiness means different things to every one of us. Once you have your answer, start doing more of these things everyday and tell me how you feel afterwards.

Smooth Sailing Forever

Some days you will forget about what makes you truly happy as you get bombarded by the harsh and cruel things life will throw at you. So I encourage you to put this list somewhere visible where you can see it everyday. Constantly remind yourself of what happiness means to you and shift your mind and body towards these actions every single day. I am sure you will be much happier person after that. See you in the next one :)

Chapter 2:
How To Rid Yourself of Distraction

Distraction and disaster sound rather similar.
It is a worldwide disorder that you are probably suffering from.
Distraction is robbing you of precious time during the day.
Distraction is robbing you of time that you should be working on your goals.
If you don't rid yourself of distraction, you are in big trouble.

It is a phenomenon that most employees are only productive 3 out of 8 hours at the office.
If you could half your distractions, you could double your productivity.
How far are you willing to go to combat distraction?
How badly do you want to achieve proper time management?

If you know you only have an hour a day to work, would it help keep you focused?

Always focus on your initial reason for doing work in the first place.
After all that reason is still there until you reach your goal.

Create a schedule for your day to keep you from getting distracted.
Distractions are everywhere.
It pops up on your phone.
It pops up from people wanting to chat at work.
It pops up in the form of personal problems.
Whatever it may be, distractions are abound.

The only cure is clear concentration.
To have clear concentration it must be something you are excited about.

Smooth Sailing Forever

To have clear knowledge that this action will lead you to something exciting.

If you find the work boring, It will be difficult for you to concentrate too long.
Sometimes it takes reassessing your life and admitting your work is boring for you to consider a change in direction.

Your goal will have more than one path.
Some paths boring, some paths dangerous, some paths redundant, and some paths magical.
You may not know better until you try.
After all the journey is everything.

If reaching your goal takes decades of work that makes you miserable, is it really worth it?
The changes to your personality may be irreversible.

Always keep the goal in mind whilst searching for an enjoyable path to attain it.
After all if you are easily distracted from your goal, then do you really want it?

Ask yourself the hard questions.
Is this something you really want? Or is this something society wants for you?

Many people who appear successful to society are secretly miserable.
Make sure you are aware of every little detail of your life.
Sit down and really decide what will make you happy at the end of your life.

What work will you be really happy to do?
What are the causes and people you would be happy to serve?
How much money you want?
What kind of relationships you want?
If you can build a clear vision of this life for you, distractions will become irrelevant.
Irrelevant because nothing will be able to distract you from your perfect vision.

Is what you are doing right now moving you towards that life?
If not stop, and start doing the things what will.
It really is that simple.

Anyone who is distracted for too long from the task in hand has no business doing that task. They should instead be doing something that makes them happy.

We can't be happy all the time otherwise we wouldn't be able to recognize it.
But distraction is a clear indicator you may not be on the right path for you.
Clearly define your path and distraction will be powerless.

Chapter 3:
How to Learn Faster

Remember the saying, "You are never too old to learn something new"? Believe me, it's not true in any way you understood it.

The most reliable time to learn something new was the time when you were growing up. That was the time when your brain was in its most hyperactive state and could absorb anything you had thrown at it.

You can still learn, but you would have to change your approach to learning.

You won't learn everything, because you don't like everything going on around you. You naturally have an ego to please. So what can you do to boost your learning? Let's simplify the process. When you decide to learn something, take a moment and ask yourself this; "Will this thing make my life better? Will this fulfill my dreams? Will I benefit from it?".

If you can answer all these questions in a positive, you will pounce on the thing and you won't find anyone more motivated than you.

Learning is your brain's capability to process things constructively. If you pick up a career, you won't find it hard to flourish if you are genuinely interested in that particular skill.

Whether it be sports, singing, entrepreneurship, cooking, writing, or anything you want to pursue. Just ask yourself, can you use it to increase your creativity, your passion, your satisfaction. If you can, you will start learning it as if you knew it all along.

Your next step to learning faster would be to improve and excel at what you already have. How can you do that? It's simple yet again!

Ask yourself another question, that; "Why must I do this? Why do I need this?" if you get to answer that, you will find the fastest and effective way to the top yourself without any coaching. Why will this happen on its own? Because now you have found a purpose for your craft and the destination is clear as the bright sun in the sky.

The last but the most important thing to have a head start on your journey of learning is the simplest of them all, but the hardest to opt for. The most important step is to start working towards things.

The flow of learning is from Head to Heart to Hands. You have thought of the things you want to do in your brain. Then you asked your heart if it satisfied you. Now it's time to put your hands to work.

You never learn until you get the chance to experience the world yourself. When you go through a certain event, your brain starts to process the outcomes that could have been, and your heart tells you to give it one more try. Here is the deciding moment. If you listen to your heart right away, you will get on a path of learning that you have never seen before.

What remains now is your will to do what you have decided. And when you get going, you will find the most useful resources immediately. Use your instincts and capitalize your time. Capture every chance with sheer will and belief as if this is your final moment for your dreams to come true.

It doesn't matter if you are not the ace in the pack, it doesn't matter if you are not in your peak physical shape, it doesn't matter if you don't have the money yet. You will someday get all those things only if you had the right skills and the right moment.

For all you know, this moment right now is the most worth it moment. So don't go fishing in other tanks when you have your own aquarium. That aquarium is your body, mind, and soul. All you need is to dive deep with sheer determination and the stars are your limit.

Chapter 4:
Don't Set The Wrong Goals

Most people even though they are the most ambitious ones in their circle do not ever succeed. It's not because they are not capable. It's not because they don't have the effort and hard work for what it takes to be successful. It's certainly not because they haven't had the opportunity.

These people have a pattern for them. These people have all the right energies and all the right tools, but only the wrong motives. These people don't have the right goals.

When you set a goal, many things make you think of them. Most of the time there is an external motivation driving our goals. But why do we need someone else to realize a certain goal?

Yes, this is the biggest reason to set the wrong goals. You don't need some sense of insecurity or jealousy to be motivated and do something that you were never meant to do or become someone who you were never meant to be.

People often portray these feelings as an effort to be extra ambitious towards some pointless thing.

The majority of us don't know what we want in our lives. It is impossible to search for something meaningful when you don't have the faintest idea of anything even closer to what you want.

There are many other things wrong with our approach to setting goals. Most of us procrastinate. We exaggerate things beyond the point of achieving. What we don't realize is that when we are not able to achieve those unrealistic things, we get demotivated and start building fears and doubts. These are the biggest enemies of any success story.

Setting up goals is a process and we need to go through the process. The first step in this process is not to take anything for granted. Because isn't a single worthless thing in life.

Don't underestimate the time and don't rush. Everything happens in a due course and you cannot rush things and expect them to be perfect.

Similarly, you cannot expect to have success without going through a single failure. Failures have a big impact on our personal development. Because failures make us tough and experienced hard-working people that everyone wishes to be. So appreciate every failure and take it as a learning curve to carve out new goals with a different approach.

The final and the most essential step towards an achievable goal is to avoid setting up negative goals. If you want something, don't take the 'The Glass is half empty' approach. If you want to look good, don't aim that you want to lose fat, just imagine and aim that you want to get healthy.

Negative goals don't mean evil thoughts, but they are the wrong approach towards the right things and this is what forces us to make undesirable and emotionally hurtful goals that don't push you to be good. They rather make you stay demotivated and alone.

The last but not the least thing is to never get hasty and put too much in your basket. Take only what you can use at a certain time and by this rule, you must follow one goal at a time.

Chapter 5:
It's Okay To Feel Uncertain

We are surrounded by a world that has endless possibilities. A world where no two incidents can predict the other. A realm where we are a slave to the unpredictable future and its repercussions.

Everyone has things weighing on their mind. Some of us know it and some of us keep carrying these weights unknowingly.

The uncertainty of life is the best gift that you never wanted. But when you come to realize the opportunities that lie at every uneven corner are worth living for.

Life changes fast, sometimes in our favor and sometimes not much. But life always has a way to balance things out. We only need to find the right approach to make things easier for us and the ones around us.

Everyone gets tested once in a while, but we need to find ways to cope with life when things get messy.

The worst thing the uncertainty of life can produce is the fear in your heart. The fear to never know what to expect next. But you can never let fear rule you.

To worry about the future ahead of us is pointless. So change the question from 'What if?' to 'What will I do if.'

If you already have this question popping up in your brain, this means that you are already getting the steam off.

You don't need to fear the uncertain because you can never wreck your life in any such direction from where there is no way back.

The uncertainty of life is always a transformation period to make you realize your true path. These uncertainties make you realize the faults you might have in your approach to things.

You don't need to worry about anything unpredictable and unexpected because not everything is out of your control every time. Things might not happen in a way you anticipated but that doesn't mean you cannot be prepared for it.

There are a lot of things that are in your control and you are well researched and well equipped to go around events. So use your experience to do the damage control.

Let's say you have a pandemic at your hand which you couldn't possibly predict, but that doesn't mean you cannot do anything to work on its effects. You can raise funds for the affected population. You can try to find new ways to minimize unemployment. You can find alternate ways to keep the economy running and so on.

Deal with your emotions as you cannot get carried away with such events being driven by your feelings.

Don't avoid your responsibilities and don't delay anything. You have to fulfill every task expected of you because you were destined to do it. The results are not predetermined on a slate but you can always hope for the best be the best version of yourself no matter how bad things get.

Life provides us with endless possibilities because when nothing is certain, anything is possible. So be your own limit.

Chapter 6:
Deal With Your Fears Now

Fear is a strange thing.
Most of our fears are phantoms that never actually appear or become real,
Yet it holds such power over us that it stops us from making steps forward in our lives.
It is important to deal with fear as it not only holds you back but also keeps you caged in irrational limitations.

Your life is formed by what you think.
It is important not to dwell or worry about anything negative.
Don't sweat the small stuff, and it's all small stuff (Richard Carlson).
It's a good attitude to have when avoiding fear.

Fear can be used as a motivator for yourself.
If you're in your 30s, you will be in your 80s in 50 years, then it will be too late.
And that doesn't mean you will even have 50 years. Anything could happen.

But let's say you do, that's 50 years to make it and enjoy it.
But to enjoy it while you are still likely to be healthy, you have a maximum of 15 years to make it - minus sleep and living you are down to 3 years.
If however you are in your 40s, you better get a move on quickly.

Does that fear not dwarf any possible fears you may have about taking action now?
Dealing with other fears becomes easy when the ticking clock is staring you in the face.
Most other fears are often irrational.

We are only born with two fears, the fear of falling and the fear of load noises.
The rest have been forced on us by environment or made up in our own minds.

Smooth Sailing Forever

The biggest percentage of fear never actually happens.

To overcome fear we must stare it in the face and walk through it knowing our success is at the other side.
Fear is a dream killer and often stops people from even trying.
Whenever you feel fear and think of quitting, imagine behind you is the ultimate fear of the clock ticking away your life.

If you stop you lose and the clock is a bigger monster than any fear.
If you let anything stop you the clock will catch you.

So stop letting these small phantoms prevent you from living,
They are stealing your seconds, minutes, hours , days and weeks.
If you carry on being scared, they will take your months, years and decades.
Before you know it they have stolen your life.

You are stronger than fear but you must display true strength that fear will be scared.
It will retreat from your path forever if you move in force towards it because fear is fear and by definition is scared.

We as humans are the scariest monsters on planet Earth.
So we should have nothing to fear
Fear tries to stop us from doing our life's work and that is unacceptable.
We must view life's fears as the imposters they are, mere illusions in our mind trying to control us.

We are in control here.
We have the free will to do it anyway despite fear.
Take control and fear will wither and disappear as if it was never here.
The control was always yours you just let fear steer you off your path.

Fear of failure, fear of success, fear of what people will think.

Smooth Sailing Forever

All irrational illusions.
All that matters is what you believe.
If your belief and faith in yourself is strong , fear will be no match for your will.

Les Brown describes fear as false evidence appearing real.
I've never seen a description so accurate.
Whenever fear rears its ugly head, just say to yourself this is false evidence appearing real.

Overcoming fear takes courage and strength in one's self.
We must develop more persistence than the resistance we will face when pursuing our dreams.
If we do not develop a thick skin and unwavering persistence we will be beaten by fear, loss and pain.

Our why must be so important that these imposters become small in comparison.
Because after all the life we want to live does dwarf any fears or set back that might be on the path.
Fear is insignificant.
Fear is just one thing of many we must beat into the ground to prove our worth.
Just another test that we must pass to gain our success.

Because success isn't your right,
You must fight
With all your grit and might
Make it through the night and shine your massive light on the world.
And show everyone you are a star.

Chapter 7:
If You Commit to Nothing, You'll Be Distracted By Everything

I don't think anyone in their right mind would like to face a challenge where they have a chance to face failure or even a possibility of it.

We all need a new lesson to learn. A lesson of commitment and conviction. A lesson of integrity, grit, and sheer will. One might ask, why should I adopt the features of a soldier rather than a normal social being. Why do I need to go to extremes?

The answer to these questions is simple yet heavy, with a load most people avoid their whole life.

We all have somewhat similar goals. We all want to be in a better place in better shape. We all want wealth. We all want healthy stable relationships. We all want respect and a million other things.

Ask yourself this; Have you ever actually tried hard enough for any of this to happen. Have you ever tried to dig deep till you found your last breath? But it felt good because you had a good enough reason and passion to pursue?

The goals of life are a compulsion to have. We all must have something to strive for. Something worth fighting for. Something we can look back and be happy about.

But having a goal and committing to it are two different things.

One can have a goal and still not be motivated enough to do anything in their power to achieve that thing. No matter how the road takes turns.

We need to have the inspiration to drive us through the rough patches of life. To make us keep pushing even if we get squeezed within the incidents happening around us.

Don't take this the wrong way but you have to accept the fact that whatever you are feeling has nothing to do with what you want to achieve. Because what you want to achieve is something that your life depends on. The goals you set aren't some wishes or a feeling that your gut gives you. These goals are the requirements of life with which you can finally say lived a happy successful life. And this statement is the ultimate purpose of your life.

You were given this life because you had the energy to go for things that weren't easy, but you had the potential to achieve these. All you needed was a little commitment and Zero distractions.

The commitment you need isn't a feeling that goes and on and off like a switch. Rather a distinct key for the lock of your life.

So if you still think you will have days where you can try one more time, Let me be clear; You better start thinking about the future of your next generation. Because I don't think they'd have one.

You need to be committed enough to do anything that takes you closer and closer to your goals and nothing that wastes a second out of your life.

Because either you go all in or you walk the line and hedge your bets. The bet here being your life.

Chapter 8:
How To Improve Your Communication Skills

Today we're going to talk about a topic that could help you be a better communicator with your spouse, your friends, and even your colleagues and bosses. Being able to express yourself fluently and eloquently is a skill that is incredibly important as it allows us to express our thoughts and ideas freely and fluently in ways that others might understand.

When we are able to communicate easily with others, we are able to build instant rapport with them and this allows us to appear better than we actually are. We may be able to cover some of our flaws if we are able to communicate our strengths better.

So how do we actually become better communicators? I believe that the easiest way to begin is to basically start talking with more people. It is my experience that after spending much time on my own without much social interaction, that i saw my standard of communication dropped quite drastically. You see, being able to talk well is essentially a social skill, and without regular practice and use, you just simply can't improve it. I saw that with irregular use of social interaction, the only skill that actually improved for me was texting. And we all know that texting is a very impersonal way to communicate and does not actually translate to real world fluency in person to person conversations.

Similarly, watching videos on communication and reading tips and tricks really does not help at all unless you apply it in the real world. And to have regular practice, you need to start by either inviting all your friends out to a meal so that you can strike up conversations and improve from there, or by maybe joining a social interaction group class of sorts that would allow you to practice verbal communication skills. If u were to ask me, I believe that making the effort to speak to your friends and colleagues is the best way to begin. And you can even ask them for feedback if there are any areas that they find you could improve on. Expect genuine feedback and criticisms as they go if you hope to improve, and do not take them personally.

It is with my personal experience that i became extremely rusty when it came to talking to friends at one point in my life, when i was sort of living in isolation. I find it hard to connect even with my best friend, and i found it hard to find topics to discuss about, mainly because i wasn't really living much to begin with, and there was nothing i was experiencing in life that was really worth sharing. If you stop living life, you stop having significant moments, you stop having problems that need solving, and you stop having friends that needs supporting. I believe the best way is to really try to engage the person you are talking to by asking them very thoughtful questions and by being genuinely interested in what they have to say. Which also coincidentally ties into my previous video about being a good listener. which you should definitely check out if you haven't done so already.

Being a good listener is also a big part of being a good communicator. The other part being able to respond in a very insightful way that isn't patronising. We can only truly connect with the person we are talking to if we are able to first understand on an empathetic level, what they are going through, and then to reply with the same level of compassion and empathy that they require of us.

With colleagues and bosses, we should be able to strike up conversations that are professional yet natural. And being natural in the way we communicate takes practice from all the other social interactions that precede us.

I believe that being a good communicator really takes time and regular practice in order for it to come one day and just click for us. For a start, just simply try to be friendly and place yourself out of your comfort zone, only then can you start to see improvements.

I challenge each and everyone of you today who are striving to be better communicators to start asking out your friends and colleagues for coffees and dinners. Get the ball rolling and just simply start talking. Over time, it will just come naturally to you. Trust me.

Motivate Yourself

Motivation is a multibillion dollar industry.
There are many great motivational materials to help keep you motivated.
Some of the motivational material is great and should be studied and applied but this kind of motivation is what I call push, which is a good start, but in combination with pull motivation,(your personal why and reason), you can reach your goals faster.
With the use of videos, books , audio material and concentrating on your reasons, the sky really is the limit.

Using what works for you, which may be different than what works for others.

Smooth Sailing Forever

Motivation is very much personal to you.
Work with what pulls you and pushes you to reach your goals on record time.
Pushing and pulling everyday until your dream becomes reality.
The pull is your WHY , the big reason for taking action in the first place.

The pull is the motivations that effect you personally, and the big fire that will help your dream burn , even through the storms and the rain.
Using the push motivators in conjunction to maximize your motivation on all fronts.
Create as much of your dream around you as you can with what you have right now to make it seem more real.
Pictures , music , videos, foods, smells , clothing.
Whatever you can do to create it now.
The engine to drive you there may not have arrived yet, but don't close the factory, work on the interior and bodywork, because your engine is on the way.
You know what you want, you know the first steps, take them in confidence, not fear.
If the dream is here, it is already real if you just believe and move towards it.

With motivation , self determination and faith you have already won the race before it has even begun.
Setting up the ideal environment for the garden of your life to flourish.
Strengthen the desire, strengthen the belief.

Motivation in the mind without belief in the heart will only lead to disappointment.

Your why must be something close to the heart for you to endure the tribulations of champions.

Your motivations must be clear and personal.

Defining your purpose, often money alone will not make us happy.

The money must have a greater personal purpose to bring you happiness.

Giving often feels more rewarding than recieving.

As living a truthful life is more rewarding than decieving.

The key to your dreams is often what you are believing.

Believing in yourself and your capabilities is key.

You can study every bit of motivational material ever made, but if you don't believe in yourself, you can not be successful.

Self belief and self motivation are far stronger than the push of what we can learn from the outside.

Let the outside information light the fire as it is intended, be a keen learner of what is relevant, and motivate yourself by concentrating on what is important to you.

Motivate yourself, health, happiness and wealth.

Its possible for you now.

If you believe and push to achieve.

Chapter 9: Overcoming Tiredness and Lethargy

Tiredness and lethargy has become a major problem for youths and adults these days. As our lives get busier and our ability to control our sleep gets more out of hand, we all face a constant struggle to stay alert and engaged in our life's work every single day. And this problem hits me as well.

You see, many of us have bad sleep habits, and while it might feel good to stay up late every night to watch Netflix and binge on YouTube and Instagram posts, we pay for it the next day by being a few hours short of a restful night when our alarm wakes us up abruptly every morning.

We tell ourselves that not needing so much sleep is fine for us, but our body tells us a different story. And we can only fake being energetic and awake for so long. Sooner or later we will no doubt experience the inability to function on an optimal level and our productivity and mood will also be affected accordingly. And this would also lead to overall tiredness and lethargy in the long run.

Before we talk about what we can do to counter and fix this problem that we have created for ourselves, we first have to understand why we consciously allow ourselves to become this tired in the first place.

I believe that many of us choose entertainment over sleep every night is because we are in some ways or another overworked to the point that we don't have enough time to ourselves every single day that we choose to sacrifice our sleep time in order to gain back that few hours of quality personal time. After spending a good 10 hours at our jobs from 9-6pm, and after settling down from the commute home and factoring in dinner time, we find ourselves with only a solid 1-2 hours of time to watch our favourite Netflix shows or YouTube, which i believe is not very much time for the average person.

When presented with the choice of sleep versus another episode or two of our guilty pleasure, it becomes painfully obvious which is the "better" choice for us. And we either knowingly or unknowingly choose entertainment and distraction over health.

Basically, I believe the amount of sleep you choose to give yourself is directly proportionate to how happy you are about your job. Because if you can't wait to get up each and everyday to begin your life's work, you will give yourself the best possible sleep you can each night to make sure you are all fired up the next day to crush your work. But conversely, if you hate your job and you feel like you have wasted all your time at work all day, you will ultimately feel that you will need to claim that time back at night to keep yourself sane and to keep yourself in the job no matter how much you dislike it. Even if it means sacrificing precious sleep to get there.

So I believe the real question is not how can we force ourselves to sleep earlier every night to get the 8 hours of sleep that we need in order not to feel tired and lethargic, but rather is there anything we can change about how we view our job and work that we come home at the end of the day feeling recharged and fulfilled to the extend that we don't have to look for a way to escape every night into the world of entertainment just to fill our hearts.

When you have found something you love to do each day, you will have no trouble going to bed at 10pm each night instead of 1 or 2am.

So I challenge each and everyone of you to take a hard look at WHY you are not getting enough sleep. There is a high chance that it could boil down to the reason I have described here today, and maybe a change in careers might be something to consider. But if you believe that this tiredness and lethargy is born out of something medical and genetic, then please do go see a doctor to get a medical solution to it.

Otherwise, take care and I wish you all the best in reclaiming back your energy to perform at your peak levels of success. See you in the next one.

Chapter 10:
Bounce Back From Failure

Failure is a big word. It is a negative word most say. It is cursed in most cases. It is frowned upon when it is on your plate. But why?

Sure, it certainly doesn't feel good when you encounter failure. We can't even forgive ourselves for failing at a simple card game. We get impatient, we get hopeless and ultimately we get depressed on even the smallest of failure we go through in everyday life.

Why is it that way? Why can't we try to change a failure into something better? Why can't we just leave that failure right there and not try to make a big deal out of each and every small little setback?

These questions have a very deep meaning and a very important place in everyone's life.

Let's start with the simplest step to make it easy for yourself to deal with a certain failure. Whenever you fail at anything, just pause for a second and talk to yourself.

Rewind what you just went through. Talk to yourself through the present circumstances. Think about what you could have done to improve at what you just did. Think about what you could have done to prevent whatever tragic incident you went through. Or what you could have done to do better at what you felt like failing at.

These questions will immediately sketch a scenario in front of your eyes. A scenario where you can actually see yourself flourishing and doing your best against all odds.

Whatever happened to you, I am sure you didn't deserve it. But so what if you

Lost some money or a loved one or your pet? Ask yourself this, is it the end of the world? Have you stopped breathing? Have you no reason left to keep living?

You had, you have, and you will always have a new thing, a new person a new place to start with. Life has endless possibilities for you to find. But you just have to bounce back from whatever setback you think you cannot get out of.

Take for example the biggest tech billionaires in the world. I am giving this example because people tend to relate more to these examples these days. Elon Musk started his carrier with a small office with his brother and they both lived in the same office for a whole year. They couldn't even afford a small place for themselves to rent.

There was a time when Elon had to decide to split his last set of investments between two companies. If he had invested in one, the other would have gone down for sure, just to give a chance to the other company to maybe become their one big hit. Guess what, he ended up keeping them both because he invested in both.

Why did he succeed? Was it because he wasn't afraid? No!

He succeeded because he had Faith after all the failures he had faced. He knew that if he kept trying against all odds and even the obvious risks, he will ultimately succeed at something for what he worked so hard for all this time!

PART 3

Chapter 1:
The Struggle With Time

Today we're going to talk about a topic that isn't commonly looked at in depth. But it is one that we might hopefully find a new appreciation for. And that is TIME.

Time is a funny thing, we are never really aware of it and how much of a limited resource it really is until we get a rude awakening. Most commonly when our mortality is tested. Whether it be a health scare, an accident, a death of a loved one, a death of a pet, we always think we have more time before that. That we will always have time to say i love you, to put off the things we always told ourselves we needed to do, to start making that change, to spend time with the people that mean the most to us.

As we go about our days, weeks and months, being bothered and distracted by petty work, by our bosses, colleagues, trying to climb the corporate ladder, we forget to stop and check in on our fiends and family... We forget that their time may be running out, and that we may not have as much time with them as we think we do, until it is too late, and then we regret not prioritising them first. All the money that we made could not ever buy back the time we have lost with them. And that is something we have to live with if we ever let that happen.

The other funny thing about time is that if we don't set it aside for specific tasks, if we don't schedule anything, we will end up wasting it on something mindless. Whether it be browsing social media endlessly, or bingeing on television, we will never run out of things to fill that time with. Can you imagine that even though time is so precious, we willingly sacrifice and trade it in for self isolation in front of our TVs and computers for hours on end. Sometimes even for days? Or even on mobile games. Some being so addictive that it consumes most of our waking hours if we are not careful.

Smooth Sailing Forever

Our devices have become dangerous time wasters. It is a tool Shea its literally sapping the living energy out of us. Which is why some responsible companies have started implementing new features that help us keep track of our screen time. To keep us in check, and to not let our children get sucked into this black hole that we might struggle to climb out of.

I believe the biggest struggle with time that we all have is how to spend it in such a way that we can be happy without feeling guilty. Guilty of not spending it wisely. And I believe the best way to start is to start defining the things that you need to do, and the things that you want to do. And then striking a balance. To set equal amounts of time into each activity so that it doesn't overwhelm or underwhelm you. Spend one hour on each activity each day that you feel will have an impact on your life in a meaningful way, and you can spend your time on television or games without remorse.

So I challenge each of you to make the most of your time. SPending time with loved ones always come first, followed by your goals and dreams, and then leisure activities. Never the other way around. That way you can be at the end of your life knowing that you had not wasted the most precious commodity that we are only given a finite amount of. Money can't buy back your youth, your health, or time with loved ones, so don't waste it.

I believe in each and everyone of you, take care, and as always ill see you in the next one.

Chapter 2:
Friendship The Key To Happiness

Today we're going to talk about the power of friendship and why i believe everyone needs to have at least 1 or 2 close friends in their lives to make life actually meaningful and worth living.

You see, for many years while i was working hard towards my goals, i spent almost all of my time on my business and little to zero time on building Long lasting relationships. And this one sided approach to success left me with a hole that weakened me emotionally, but also physically as well.

In this very myopic view of what I felt success should be and what I felt i needed to do at that point, I prioritised my career first over everything else, neglecting my own personal health, family, and friends. Whenever I was invited for a meal or an outing I always declined, viewing that it was a waste of time. That it was taking time away from my work that i should be focusing on. And as I declined more and more of these offers from friends, the invite also became less and less frequent as they saw me as someone who was either too busy, or just didn't bother to want to take this friendship to the next level.

For a while I was actually happy, that i remember telling myself that yes I dont have plans for the week and that i can focus on my work wholeheartedly. But what i failed to realise was that I was prioritise making money over everything else. And that i was losing the connection with other humans. I started to become more withdrawn, more introverted, and I was losing that spark that i once had when conversing with friends. I wasn't experiencing life enough to have any meaningful moments that I could look back on and say that wow those were great times.

Smooth Sailing Forever

It all became one giant blur and 3 years later, it felt truly pointless. I found myself lonely and without someone I could talk to. I even neglected my best friend to the point that we drifted so far apart that she found other people to confide into. This left me with a sinking feeling that I had failed to prioritise The people around me.

And from that point on I knew i needed to change. I knew i needed to put myself out there once again and shift my priorities to the things that truly mattered. Friends that could ask you out for a quick meal so that you could hash out some of your grievances in life, friends that you can share your happiness as well as your sadness, friends that could provide some meaning to the days you were living, and even more simply, friends that you can count on when all else fails.

You see the business that I spent 3 years building collapsed on me. And I found myself with nothing to show for it. No experiences worth highlighting. Only regrets that I had failed to put others before my selfish needs.

It was a hard climb back to establishing the friendships I once had. People had already started viewing me as a flaker and a no-show that it was now up to me to prove to them that I was open and available to be called a reliable friend once again. Some efforts on my part did not go as I had planned but I kept trying to make new connections, joining new groups, making tennis friends, starting up conversations with new people and asking if they could invite me along to an outing. And these little seeds started to show fruition. I soon found myself getting asked out for meals and games, and life started to feel a little bit better again.

After the initial struggle, the floodgates starting opening and I found myself busy with true life again, connecting with other people on a deep personal and emotional level. And i felt that that was what life was really all about. Friends that you can see yourself hanging out 40 years down the road when you are old and nobody wants you anymore.

Smooth Sailing Forever

I plan to keep sowing these seeds for as long as life allows me and I challenge each and everyone of you to do the same. Businesses and careers may not last, but hopefully the friends that you have made will.

Take care and I'll see you in the next one.

Chapter 3:
Get in the Water (Stop wasting time)

Stop wasting time.

If you have something to do, then do it. It is literally that simple. Nobody likes something hanging over their head, it is stressful and pressurising and the longer you leave it, the more of a challenge it is going to be. Just get it done.

It's like getting into cold water. You can start by dipping your big toe in, then walking away and reconsidering, before putting all five of them in, maybe if you are feeling frisky you'll put in your whole foot. It is such a waste. You know you are going to get in the water eventually so you might as well dive in. Otherwise, you will spend 80% of your time drawing out an adjustment that could literally take a few seconds. What is the point? Just dive in and get it over with. Does it take a bigger first-off effort, yes. But it saves you so much time and energy afterwards. After the initial shock and a few seconds of feeling like your skin is trying to shrivel up, you are fine.

If we can do it with cold water then we can do it with that email, project or book. You can dive right into all that research you need to do. Yes, it seems overwhelming, and that first leap is going to be full of questions and discomfort. Mid-air you will probably be asking what you got yourself into but the great thing is that you can't stop mid-air. There's no turning around and floating on the air until you reach solid ground again. You are committed now.

The powerful thing is that 90% percent of your problem is inertia. It is that first step. It's sitting down, firing up your laptop and starting to work. It is getting past the idea that you have so much work to do and just focussing on what you can do right now. But when it comes down it you must realise that there is no work around for that. You cannot not do that first step. Even if it is just a passion you know that passion is going to keep burning you up on the inside until you allow it to burst out. There's no getting past the cold water, there is only getting into it. So you might as well jump. If you are trying to write a book, then sit down and just start typing. Even if you are not even typing words, just sit down for 25 minutes and type away at your keyboard. Then, while you are typing you will realise that you are sitting down and pressing the keys anyways so they may as well say something that make sense. I don't care if what you type is cliché because at this point we are not worried about quality. I don't care how good your form is in your butterfly stroke if you are not even in the water. You just need to get started so that you are moving. And once you are moving you can maximise on your momentum.

Chapter 4:
When It Is Time To Let Go and Move On (Career)

Today we're going to talk about a topic that I hope will motivate you to quit that job that you hate or one that you feel that you have nothing more to give anymore.

For the purpose of this video, we will focus mainly on career as I believe many of you may feel as though you are stuck in your job but fear quitting because you are afraid you might not find a better one.

For today's topic, I want to draw attention to a close friend of mine who have had this dilemma for years and still hasn't decided to quit because he is afraid that he might not get hired by someone else.

In the beginning of my friend's career, he was full of excitement in his new job and wanted to do things perfectly. Things went pretty smoothly over the course of the first 2 years, learning new things, meeting new friends, and getting settled into his job that he thought he might stay on for a long time to come seeing that it was the degree that he had pursued in university. However when the 3rd year came along, he started to feel jaded with his job. Everyday he would meet ungrateful and sometimes mean customers who were incredibly self-entitled. They would be rude and he started dreading going to work more and more each day. This aspect of the job wore him down and he started to realise that he wasn't happy at all with his work.

Having had a passion for fitness for a while now, he realized that he felt very alive when he attended fitness classes and enjoyed working out and teaching others how to work out. He would fiddle with the idea of attending a teacher training course that would allow him to be a professional and certified fitness coach.

As his full time job started to become more of a burden, he became more serious about the prospect of switching careers and pursuing a new one entirely. At his job, realized that the company wasn't generous at all with the incentives and gruelling work hours, but he stayed on as he was afraid he wouldn't find another job in this bad economy. The fear was indeed real so he kept delaying trying to quit his job. Before he knew it 3 years more had passed and by this time he full on dreaded every single minute at his job.

It was not until he made that faithful decision one day to send in his resignation letter and to simultaneously pay for the teacher training course to become a fitness instructor did his fortunes start to change for him. The fortunes in this wasn't about money. It was about freedom. It was about growth. And it was about living.

We all know deep in our hearts when it is time to call it quits to something. When we know that there is nothing more that we can possibly give to our job. That no amount of time more could ever fulfill that void in us. That we just simply need to get out and do something different.

You see, life is about change. As we grow, our priorities change, our personalities change, our expectations change, and our passions and our interests change as well. If we stay in one place too long, especially in a field or in something that we have hit a wall at, we will feel stuck, and we will feel dread. We will feel that our time spent is not productive and we end up feeling hopeless and sorry for ourselves.

Instead when we choose to let go, when we choose to call time on something, we open up the doors for time on other ventures, and other adventures. And our world becomes brighter again.

Smooth Sailing Forever

I challenge each and everyone of you to take a leap of faith. You know deep in your hearts when it is time to move on from your current job and find the next thing. If you dont feel like you are growing, or if you feel that you absolutely hate your job because there is no ounce of joy that you can derive from it, move on immediately. Life is too short to be spending 10 hours of your life a day on something that you hate, that sucks the living soul out of you. Give yourself the time and space to explore, to find some other path for you to take. You will be surprised what might happen when you follow your heart.

I hope you learned something today, take care and I'll see you in the next one.

Chapter 5:
Being Open To Opportunities For Social Events

As we continue from the previous video, something I learned is that things never turn out as how you would expect to in life. And the more we try to force something, the more resistance we face. And the more we take things in stride and just trust the process, the more things tend to flow naturally. You will see what I mean as we go through this video together.

As I was describing about how my social life was basically non existent at one point, if you guys haven't watched that video, do check it out first.

After taking a hard look at the decisions I made that left me with little to no social support or events to go to, i knew that I needed to do a 180 if i hoped to see any sort of rebound in my social life. And I started making a concrete plan with specific actions that would put me in a favourable position to attract and keep new friends.

At my lowest point, I knew that there was little that I could do to salvage my previous relationships, that I had probably done irreparable harm to them and i needed to start all over again. And that is to Make new friends from scratch. It wasn't so much something that I felt i needed right away, but i knew that in the long run, investing in friendships would bring me much more joy than money ever could especially in the latter years of my life. I knew that money wasn't the end all be all, and that people was the way to go.

Money can be made, but friendships cannot be bought.

Smooth Sailing Forever

I started the goal of dedicating this year and beyond to new friendships and began by signing up for activities that were in line with my interests. As an avid tennis fan and a player of the game, i decided that that was where i would begin. I started joining tennis groups and started playing games with complete strangers. Having also a growing interest in yoga and working out, I also started going for classes with my membership. Whilst i did not really make any real friends right away, I felt that I was already connected in some ways to people with similar interests. And I felt like i was part of a community, that I belonged somewhere. The more i showed up for these activities, the more people kept seeing me around, and the more these people started associated me as being regulars. Soon I was invited by one or two people to join a private game and that in itself became a regular thing. I started seeing these faces weekly for a year and we became friends naturally over the game of tennis. Yoga was a different story as it was more of an individual kind of sport, and people were generally more focused on their own practice on the mat, but it was fine as my interest for yoga faded pretty quickly anyway.

At the gym I started making one or two friends as well. It became natural to chat up with the gym regulars and even the staff, i felt like i looked forward to attending these events not because I wanted to work out, but because I enjoyed the social part and meeting my new friends and striking up random conversations.

For those of you who work in 9-5 jobs, you might not face this same issue as me, as meeting new people and colleagues would be a very simple way to start making new aquaintances that could potentially turn into friends... Seeing that you would meet them every single day whether you liked it or not. But for people who work from home or who are self employed, we do need to make the extra effort to meet new people.

As my pool of friends grew bigger, I started forming my own private tennis group, putting in the extra effort to book the courts day in and out, and inviting them to play. Eventually all my hard work paid off, as people reciprocated by inviting me to their own private outings and dinners. And I started to integrate into their lives and their friends. I had made myself so readily available, not by design, but by choice because at that point

Smooth Sailing Forever

I was so ready to say yes to anything it became so natural to prioritise hanging out over just simply working all day and night. My friends saw me as someone they could count on to be there and they had no qualms making me a priority when they wanted to find somebody to hang out with. I reciprocated by making them a priority as well. And the friendship blossomed from there.

For the first time in a long time, I felt truly alive. I felt that my life had a purpose, it had balance, it had work and play, there was yin to my yang, and i looked forward to working as much as I looked forward to hanging out.

I don't know how long this bliss will last, but i know that I had made the right choice. This all happened in 2020, smack in the middle of the pandemic, and yet I made it work because I had given myself every opportunity to succeed.

If this story resonated with you, then i challenge each and everyone of you today to simply decide on a time and place you would like to begin changing the areas of your life that you find lacking. The one thing that I have learned from all this is that it is never tooo late to turn things around. Whether it be financial, emotional, or physical. A firm decision to change is all it takes. And giving it time to grow and blossom is essential to seeing long term success.

I hope you have learned something today and I wish you all the best in putting yourself in positions where opportunities would arise. Take care and I'll see you in the next one.

Chapter 6:
Trust The Process

Today we're going to talk about the power of having faith that things will work out for you even though you can't see the end in sight just yet. And why you need to simply trust in the process in all the things that you do.

Fear is something that we all have. We fear that if we quit our jobs to pursue our passions, that we may not be able to feed ourselves if our dreams do not work out. We fear that if we embark on a new business venture, that it might fail and we would have incurred financial and professional setbacks.

All this is borne out of the fear of the unknown. The truth is that we really do not know what can or will happen. We may try to imagine in our heads as much as we can, but we can never really know until we try and experienced it for ourselves.

The only way to overcome the fear of the unknown is to take small steps, one day at a time. We will, to the best of our ability, execute the plan that we have set for ourselves. And the rest we leave it up to the confidence that our actions will lead to results.

If problems arise, we deal with it there and then. We put out fires, we implement updated strategies, and we keep going. We keep going until we have exhausted all avenues. Until there is no more roads for us to travel, no more paths for us to create. That is the best thing that we can do.

If we constantly focus on the fear, we will never go anywhere. If we constantly worry about the future, we will never be happy with the present. If we dwell on our past failures, we will be a victim of our own shortcomings. We will not grow, we will not learn, we will not get better.

I challenge each and every one of you today to make the best out of every situation that you will face. Grab fear by the horns and toss them aside as if it were nothing. I believe in you and all that you can achieve.

Removing The Things In Your Day That Don't Serve A Purpose for You

Today I went to a yoga class and felt that something was not quite right. I did not enjoy it as much as I used to. As I was acting out the poses that the teacher was instructing to us, i found myself wondering what the heck I was doing on my yoga mat. Something i used to look forward everyday suddenly became a chore to me, and I didn't understand why.

I had been forcing myself for the past month thinking that I needed the class to stretch and to feel more flexible. But the more i attended, the unhappier I was. And it was only after I decided to completely remove yoga from my itinerary did I feel my day was actually more enjoyable.

Many times we plan things in our day just for the sake of it. We plan things because we think we have to, even if it didn't bring much joy into our lives.

I would like you to think of some of the things in your week, what are those that don't bring joy to you? Could you replace them with something that you might find a little more enjoyable instead?

i believe that many of us try to pack so much into our schedule thinking that the busier we are, the more meaningful our lives are, the more we are getting out of it. While it might be true to a certain extent, over doing and over subscribing can actually be counter-productive for us. All of us need rest and relaxation to recharge and tackle the next day. If we are packing our schedule of things we hate, we will never truly be at peace in life. It is okay to stop the things that stop bringing you joy, and maybe coming back to it at a later time.

I found myself loving to spend time stretching by myself while listening to music rather than doing it in a yoga class. And as soon as I replaced this block of time with something that I enjoyed, it made my day that much better, even if it was just a little.

Start taking a hard look at everything we are putting our time, energy, and commitment to, what are the areas that we should trim that don't serve us anymore, and how can we either replace them with something better or just freeing up time to rest and sleep instead until we figure it out.

You may find yourself just a little bit happier.

Chapter 7:
Pressures of Social Media

Ah social media. This piece of technology has he power to either make us better people and more connected, or wreck us all completely. I want to address this topic today because I feel that social media is a tool that has uses that can impact us either negatively or positively, depending on how we use it. For the purpose of this video, we will talk about how social media can affect our self-worth and self-esteem.

For most of us, when we first hop onto social media, our goal is to connect with our friends. We hop onto Facebook and Instagram to add our friends and to see what's up in their lives, and to be involved with them digitally so to speak. We start by chatting them up and checking out their photos and posts. And we feel happy to be part of a bigger network.

However sooner or later, we get sucked into the pressure of acquiring more people to boost our profile... to get more likes... to get more followers... to become... famous. And every time we post something, we always feel inferior that we don't have as many likes as our friends. That we are somehow unpopular. Furthermore, we start comparing our lives with our friends, and we see what a wonderful life they have lived, the amazing photos that they have taken around the world, and we start wondering where we had gone wrong in our lives, and why we are in such a "terrible" state. We start to wonder if we had made a mistake in our career paths and we constantly compare ourselves to others that make ourselves feel Low.

Another pressure we face from social media is in the area of body image and self-worth. We see posts of the world of the insta-famous, their chiseled bodies, their chiseled faces, their amazing hair, amazingly toned skin and beauty standards that we just can't help but compare ourselves to. We start feeling inferior and we start to think we are not beautiful. We then look for ways to improve the way we look that always makes us feel so lousy about ourselves. What's more is that we come across posts of people with amazing houses and with money beyond our wildest imaginations and we again beat ourselves up for it. We wonder why we are not in that same place in life as them.

Every time we open the app to see these accounts, this regular and constant comparisons leaves us with terrible Low self-esteem and self-worth that manifests in us day in and day out. And over time, it becomes part of our negative outlook on our own lives.

I had subjected myself to a few of these before when I first started out on social media. It became all too easy to bow to the pressure of social media when all you are feeding your mind every single day is the same exactly self-harming thing.

It was only after I took a break from social media and had time to grow up a little bit that I started to use social media in a much healthier way.

After coming back to social media after a long hiatus, I stopped chasing likes, stop chasing new followers, and focused on merely reconnecting once again with my friends. I stopped browsing random accounts that will always get me lost in this rabbit hole and I felt much better about myself. As I grew up, I stopped comparing myself to others but rather view people who are in better places than I was as ways to inspire me. I started to fill my accounts with people that would inspire me to get me where I want to be whether it be financially or physically. This profound shift in the way I used social media actually got me fired up each day to work towards my goals.

Using social media as a tool of inspiration, I found myself excited to start making more money from each of my followers' inspirational posts. Whether it be from following tony-Robbins, accounts created by warren buffet followers, to people who were successful in YouTube and other online business platforms, I was motivated every time I logged in rather than leaving feeling worthless.

Smooth Sailing Forever

Who you follow matters and how you choose to use social media matters as well. If you choose comparison rather than inspiration, you will always feel like you are unworthy. If you view other's success as a motivator, you can choose to follow people that inspire you each and every day to get you where you want to go.

I challenge each and every one of you to align your goals with social media. Think hard about what you want to use it for. Is it a means of escape? Or is it a tool for you to get cracking on your goals. If you wish to be healthier, follow people who inspire you each day to start working out rather than those that posts photos that only serve to show off their physique. If you want to be richer, following successful people who teach you life principles to be wealthy, rather than accounts that merely show off their incredible wealth with things they buy and the branded stuff they own. If you goal is to be a better person, there are plenty of accounts that seek to inspire. Maybe Oprah Winfrey would be a good person to o follow, if she has an account.

Choose who you follow wisely because their daily posts will have a direct consequences to how you start seeing things around you.

Chapter 8:
Share Your Wisdom with the World

Today we're going to talk about how to share your wisdom with the world. How many of you think that you have something meaningful to share with others? Whether you are an expert at a particular field, or just that you are particularly good at a certain task.

Have you ever thought about putting your knowledge out there so that people can learn from you?

It is incredibly powerful the gifts that you and I possess. We all have different talents, wisdom, knowledge, that are unique to each individual. No 2 humans are the same, and that goes the same for what they have to offer. What you have to give is uniquely special to you and you only.

I want to bring light to this topic because I too was once afraid to let my voice be heard. I felt that I had no authority, certification, or whatever qualification to be able to write on relationships or about life. I always thought that what I had to say maybe wasn't that important, that it wouldn't help anybody. But i soon realized that it was my own limiting beliefs about myself that were holding me back from sharing my truth with the world.

As I leaned in to more about personal development, I opened my eyes to the wonderful possibilities that we all have to offer as humans. I started to believe that maybe I had something worth sharing. That maybe an article that i wrote or a video that i put out, or an audiobook that i published could help someone somewhere, somehow.

I started to believe that as long as I can change 1 life, that would be good enough a reason for me to spend my time and energy into publishing something that would go out there into the world. Yeah there will be haters. Yes there will be people telling me that what I say is stupid or doesn't make sense, but as long as I believed in what i had to say, it was all that mattered.

We all have a right to share our truth. That truth may not sit well with everyone, but you will find your audience. If you have something to say, put it out there. Help someone in need.

Social media and the internet has become such a powerful force that everything we share can be instantaneously broadcasted all over the world. Think of that kind of power. If you have a powerful voice, a positive one, share it.

that is my challenge for each and everyone of you today. To believe in yourself, your wisdom, and not be afraid to show it to the world.

The Power of Community

The topic that we are going to discuss today is something that I feel has resonated with me one a more personal level recently. And it is one that I have largely neglected in the past.

As i have mentioned before in other videos, that as an entrepreneur of sorts, my job required me to work independently, mostly from home. And while it may sound nice to others, or even yourself, where you think it is a privilege to work from home, many a times it is actually not all that fun because there is no sense of community or interaction with others. And the job becomes quite lonesome.

I'm sure many of you who have experienced lockdowns and Work from home situations, that it may seem fun for a week, but after that you realize that actually it isn't all that it is cracked out to be. And you actually do wanna get dressed, get out of the house, and go somewhere to do your work rather than stay in your PJs all day and waste your time away.

But if you dig deeper, you will realize that what you actually miss is the interaction with your co-workers, to just walk over to their desk to ask them something, or simply to just start a conversation because maybe you're bored, or to have lunch together instead of cooking your own instant noodles at home.

As social creatures, we crave that human interaction. And we crave belonging in a community and being a part of something bigger than ourselves.

When we are in lockdown, we lose that personal touch that we have with others, and we start to feel restless, we feel that something is missing but we can't put our finger on it. It is not the actual work at the job that we look forward to, but rather the people, the colleagues that make working fun and enjoyable.

Smooth Sailing Forever

The same goes for any sports of workout. You will realize that when you gym alone, you are less likely to show up because there is no one there to push you to make you do one more rep. There is no community to keep you going back to stick to your goals. For those of you who do yoga, i am sure the experience is very different when you practice an hour of yoga at home versus in a yoga studio with 30 other people, even if you don't know any of them. There is still a sense that you are a part of a greater unit, a class that works out together, a group of like-minded individuals who really want the same thing and share the same interests. You feel compelled to go back because the community is there to make the exercise fun. That after a tiring workout you look to the people beside and around you and you see the same expressions on their faces. That they had shared an activity with you and feel the same things. Isn't that what life is really about? To be a part of something rather than going about it like a lone wolf?

So for those of you who feel like something is amiss in the activity that you once loved, be it a sports or a job, or an activity that you have no choice to do but never felt happy doing it, i challenge you to find a like-minded community who share the same beliefs and interests. You can easily look for such groups on meet-up apps. You might find that the missing puzzle is indeed other individuals that share your likes. And when you work around them or with them, you will feel a much greater sense of joy and happiness that you never thought you could feel.

I hope you learned something today and I'll see you in the next one. Take care.

Chapter 9:
The Lure of Wanting Luxury Items

Have you ever walked by a store and pondered over those LV bags if you were a lady? Secretly hoping that you can get your hands on one of those bags so that you can feel good about yourself when you carry them on your shoulders? Or have you ever glanced at a boutique watch shop if you were a guy hoping that you can get your hands on one of the rolexes which costs north of $10k minimum? That could be the same lust and desire for the latest and greatest cars, apple products, clothing, etc. anything you name it.

You think of saving up a year's worth of salary just to be able to afford one of these things and you see yourself feeling good about it and that you can brag to your friends and show off to people that you have the latest and most expensive product on the market. and you imagine yourself being happy that it is all you will need to stay happy.

I am here to tell you that the lure of owning luxury items can only make you happy to a certain extent. And only if purchasing these things is something of great meaning to you, like achieving a big milestone that you want to commemorate in life. In that instance, walking into that store to purchase that luxury product can be a great experience and of great significance as well. Whether it be a birthday gift to yourself, or commemorating a wedding anniversary, job/career work milestone, or any of that in nature, you will tend to hold these products with great sentimental value and hardly will you ever sell these items should the opportunity arise to make a profit from them (which is generally not the case with most things you buy).

I will argue that when you pick these products to wear from your wardrobe, you will indeed be filled with feelings of happiness, but it is not the product itself that makes you happy, but it is the story behind it, the hard work, the commemorative occasion that you will associate and remember these products for. It will transport you back in time to that place in your life when you made the purchase and you will indeed relive that emotion that took you there to the store in the first place. That to me is a meaningful luxury purchase that is not based on lust or greed, but of great significance.

But what if you are just someone who is chasing these luxury products just because everyone else has it? When you walk down the street and you see all these people carrying these products and you just tell yourself you have to have it or else? You find all the money you can dig from your savings and emergency fund to pay for that product? I would argue that in that instance, you will not be as happy as you thought you would be. These kinds of wants just simply do not carry the weight of any importance. And after feeling good for a few days after you owned that luxury good, you feel a deep sense of emptiness because it really does not make you a happier person. Instead you are someone trying to have something but with that comes a big hole in your wallet or your bank account. The enthusiasm and excitement starts to fade away and you wonder whats the next luxury good you need to buy to feel that joy again.

You see, material goods cannot fill us with love and happiness. Luxury goods are only there to serve one purpose, to reward you for your hard work and that you can comfortably purchase it without regret and worry that you are left financially in trouble. The lure of many of us is that we tend to want what we can't have. It could also turn into an obsession for many of us where we just keep buying more and more of these luxury goods to satisfy our craving for materialistic things. You will realise one day that the pursuit never ends, the more you see, the more you want. And that is just how our brains are wired.

I have a confession to make, I had an obsession for apple products myself and I always thought I wanted the latest and greatest apple products every year when a new model comes out. And every year apple seems to know how to satisfy my lust for these products and manages to make me spend thousands of dollars every time they launch something new. This addiction i would say lasted for a good 8 years until I recently realised that the excitement ALWAYS fades after a week or two. Sure it is exciting to play with it for a couple of days while your brain gets used to this incredible piece of technology sitting in front of you. But after a week or two, I am left wondering, whats next? I began to realise that what really made me happy was doing what i love, engaging in my favourite hobbies, meeting friends, and just living simply without so many wants in life. When you have less wants, you automatically go into a mindset of abundance. And that is a great feeling to have.

I challenge all of you today to question what is your real motivation behind wanted to buy luxury items. Is it to commemorate a significant achievement in your life? or is it a meaningless lust for something that you want to emulate others for. Dig deeper and you will find the answer. Thank you

Chapter 10:
The 5 Second Rule

Today I'm going to share with you a very special rule in life that has worked wonders for me ever since I discovered it. And that is known as the 5 second rule by Mel Robbins.

You see, on a daily basis, I struggle with motivation and getting things done. I struggle with the littlest things like replying an email, to responding to a work request. This struggle has become such a bad habit that before I think about beginning any sort of work, I would first turn on my Netflix account to watch an episode or two of my favourite sitcom, telling myself that I will get right on it after I satisfy this side of me first.

This habit of procrastination soon became so severe that I would actually sit and end up wasting 4-5 hours of time every morning before I would actually even begin on any work-related stuff. Before I knew it, it would be 3pm and I haven't gotten a single thing done. All the while I was staring at the clock, counting the number of hours I have wasted, while simultaneously addicted to procrastinating that I just could not for the life of me get myself off the couch onto my desk to begin any meaningful work.

I realized that something had to change. If I kept this up, I would not only not get anything done, like ever, but i would also begin to loathe myself for being so incredibly unproductive and useless. This process of self-loathing got worse everyday I leaned into the habit of procrastination. It was only until i stumbled onto Mel Robbin's 5 second rule that I started to see a real change in my habits.

Smooth Sailing Forever

The rule is simple, to count backwards from 5 and to just get up and go do that thing. It sounded stupid to me at first, but it worked. Instead of laying around in bed every morning checking my phone before I woke up, I would count backwards from 5 and as soon as it hit 1, i would get up and head straight towards the shower, or I would pack up my things and get out of my house.

I had identified that staying at home was the one factor that made me the most unproductive person on the planet, and that the only way I knew I was going to get real work done, was to get out of the house. I had also identified that showering was a good way to cleanse my mind from the night before. I really enjoyed showering as I always seem to have a clear head afterwards to be able to focus. What works for me, may not necessarily work for you. You have to identify for yourself when are the times you are most productive, and simply replicate it. A good way to find out is by journaling, which I will talk about in a separate video. Journaling is a good way to capture a moment in time and a particular state of mind. Try it for yourself the next time you are incredibly focused, write down how you got to that state, and simply do it again the next time to get there.

The 5 second rule is so simple yet so powerful because it snaps our unhealthy thought patterns. As Mel puts it, our brain is hardwired to protect us. We procrastinate out of fear of doing the things that are hard, so we have to beat our brain to it by disrupting it first. When we decide to move and take action after reaching 1, it is too late for our brains to stop us. And we get the ball rolling.

I was at my most productive on days that I felt my worst. But I overcame it because I didn't let my brain stop me from myself. I wouldn't say that I am struggle free now, but i knew i had a tool that would work most of the time to get me out of procrastination and into doing some serious work that would move my life forward. There are times when I would forget about the 5 second rule and my bad habits would kick in, but I always reminded myself that it was available to me if I chose to use it.

I would urge all of you who are struggling with any form of procrastination or laziness to give the 5 second rule a try. All you need to do is to get started and the rest becomes easy.

Setting Too High Expectations

Today we're going to talk about the topic of setting too high expectations. Expectations about everything from work, to income, to colleagues, friends, partners, children, family. Hopefully by the end of this video I will be able to help you take things down a notch in some areas so that you don't always get disappointed when things don't turn out the way you expect it to.

Let's go one by one in each of these areas and hopefully we can address the points that you are actively engaged in at the moment.

Let's begin with work and career. Many of us have high expectations for how we want our work life to be. How we expect our companies and colleagues to behave and the culture that we are subjected to everyday. More often that not though, companies are in the business of profit-making and cutting costs. And our high expectations may not meet reality and we might end up getting let down. What I would recommend here is that we not set these expectations of our colleagues and bosses, but rather we should focus on how we can best navigate through this obstacle course that is put in front of us. We may want to focus instead on how we can handle ourselves and our workload. If however we find that we just can't shake off this expectations that we want from working in a company, maybe we want to look elsewhere to companies that have a work culture that suits our personality. Maybe one that is more vibrant and encourages freedom of expression.

Another area that we should address is setting high expectations of our partners and children. Remember that we are all human, and that every person is their own person. Your expectations of them may not be their expectations of themselves. When you impose such an ideal on them, it may be hard for them to live up to. Sure you should expect your partner to be there for you and for your children to behave a certain way. But beyond that everyone has their own personalities and their own thoughts and ideas. And what they want may not be in line with what we want for them. Many a times for Asian parents, we expect our kids to get good grades, get into good colleges, and maybe becoming a doctor or lawyer one day. But how many of us actually understand what our kids really want? How many of us actually listen to what our kids expect of themselves? Maybe they really want to be great at music, or a sport, or even finance. Who's to say what's actually right? We should learn to trust others and let go of some of our own expectations of them and let them become whoever they want to be.

The next area I want to talk about is simply setting too high expectations of yourself. Many times we have an ideal of who we want to be - how we want to look, how we want our bodies to look, and how we want our bank statement to look, amongst many others. The danger here is when we set unrealistic expectations as to when we expect these things to happen. Remember most things in life takes time to happen. The sooner you realise that you need more time to get there, the easier it will be on yourself. When we set unrealistic timelines, while it may seem ideal to rush through the process to get results fast, more often than not we are left disappointed when we don't hit them. We then get discouraged and may even feel like a failure or give up the whole process entirely. Wouldn't it be better if we could give ourselves more time for nature to work its magic? Assuming you follow the steps that you have laid out and the action plans you need to take, just stretch this timeline out a little farther to give yourself more breathing room. If you feel you are not progressing as fast as you had hoped, it is okay to seek help and to tweak your plans as they go along. Don't ever let your high expectations discourage you and always have faith and trust in the process even when it seems hard.

Smooth Sailing Forever

One final thing I want to talk about is how we can shift from setting too high expectations to one of setting far-out goals instead. There is a difference. Set goals that serve to motivate you and inspire you to do things rather than ones that are out of fear. When we say we expect something, we immediately set ourselves up for disappoint. However if we tell ourselves that we really want something, or that we want to achieve something that is of great importance to us, we shift to a goal-oriented mindset. One that is a lot healthier. We no longer fear the deadline creeping up on us. We instead continually work on getting there no matter how long it takes. That we tell ourselves we will get there no matter what, no matter how long. The key is to keep at it consistently and never give up.

Having the desire to work at an Apple store as a retail specialist, I never let myself say that I expect apple to hire me by a certain time otherwise I am never pursuing the job ever again. Rather I tell myself that being an Apple specialist is my dream job and that I will keep applying and trying and constantly trying to improve myself until Apple has no choice but to hire me one day. A deadline no longer bothers me anymore. While I wait for them to take me in, I will continue to pursue other areas of interest that will also move my life forward rather than letting circumstances dictate my actions. I know that I am always in control of my own ship and that I will get whatever I put my mind to eventually if I try hard enough.

So with that I challenge each and every one of you to be nicer to yourselves. Lower your lofty expectations and focus on the journey instead of the deadline. Learn to appreciate the little things around you and not let your ego get in the way.

I hope you learned something today, take care and I'll see you in the next one.

www.ingramcontent.com/pod-product-compliance
Lightning Source LLC
LaVergne TN
LVHW010446070526
838199LV00066B/6227